Batty for Black

by Christianne C. Jones   illustrated by Todd Ouren

Special thanks to our advisers for their expertise:

Linda Frichtel, Design Adjunct Faculty
Minneapolis College of Art & Design

Terry Flaherty, Ph.D., Professor of English
Minnesota State University, Mankato

PICTURE WINDOW BOOKS
Minneapolis, Minnesota

Editor: Jill Kalz
Designer: Hilary Wacholz
Page Production: Melissa Kes
Art Director: Nathan Gassman
The illustrations in this book were created digitally.

Picture Window Books
151 Good Counsel Drive
P.O. Box 669
Mankato, MN 56002-0669
877-845-8392
www.picturewindowbooks.com

Printed in the United States of America.

 All books published by Picture Window Books
are manufactured with paper containing at least
10 percent post-consumer waste.

Library of Congress Cataloging-in-Publication Data
Jones, Christianne C.
Batty for black / by Christianne C. Jones ; illustrated by
Todd Ouren.
p. cm. — (Know your colors)
ISBN: 978-1-4048-3764-5 (library binding)
1. Black—Juvenile literature. 2. Colors—Juvenile literature.
I. Ouren, Todd, ill. II. Title.
QC495.5.J6557 2008
535.6—dc22   2007004271

The world is filled with COLORS.

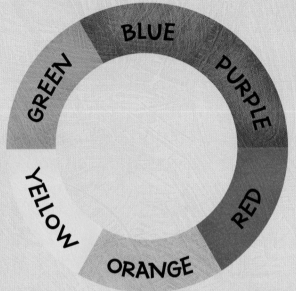

Colors are either primary or secondary. Red, yellow, and blue are primary colors. These are the colors that can't be made by mixing two other colors together. Orange, purple, and green are secondary colors. Secondary colors are made by mixing together two primary colors.

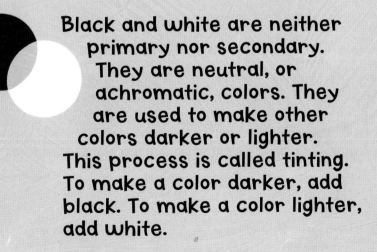

Black and white are neither primary nor secondary. They are neutral, or achromatic, colors. They are used to make other colors darker or lighter. This process is called tinting. To make a color darker, add black. To make a color lighter, add white.

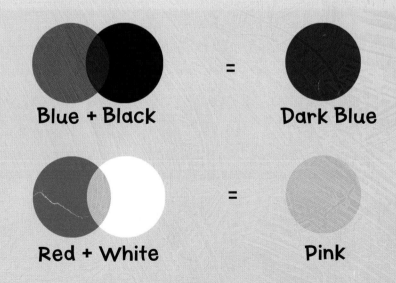

Blue + Black = Dark Blue

Red + White = Pink

Keep your eyes open for colorful fun!

3

The color **BLACK** makes a spooky scene.

It's a color that is sure to make you scream!

A long **BLACK** car drives up the hill.

Thick **BLACK** clouds bring a frightening chill.

8

9

A man in **BLACK** leads the way.

Tattered **BLACK** curtains begin to sway.

13

14

Tiny **BLACK** bats swoop low and high.

15

Two eerie **BLACK** birds keep a watchful eye.

A creepy **BLACK** spider gives everyone a scare.

19

A hissing **BLACK** cat has a crazy stare.

21

Your tour is done. Will you ever come back?
A haunted house is the place to find **BLACK**.

TINTING WITH BLACK

WHAT YOU NEED:
- red, white, and green paint
- paper plates
- black paint
- paintbrushes

WHAT YOU DO:

1. Put a quarter-sized blob of red paint on a paper plate.

2. Add a few drops of black paint to the red, and mix the colors together with a paintbrush.

3. Repeat the first two steps with the white and black paint, then the green and black. How do the colors change?

4. Now, try the activity again. This time, add just one drop of black paint to each color. How does the amount of black paint affect the colors?

FUN FACTS

- In most parts of the world, black stands for death and mourning. However, black can also mean formal and elegant.

- There are no flowers that are truly black. "Black roses" are actually very dark red, and "black tulips" are very dark purple.

- In karate and other types of martial arts, a black belt is the highest level anyone can reach. Only experts wear black belts.

- Ebony, onyx, and jet black are all words that mean "black."

TO LEARN MORE

MORE BOOKS TO READ

Dahl, Michael. *Black: Seeing Black All Around Us.* Mankato, Minn.: Capstone Press, 2005.

Murray, Julie. *Color.* Edina, Minn.: ABDO Pub., 2007.

Thomas, Isabel. *Black Foods.* Chicago: Heinemann, 2004.

ON THE WEB

FactHound offers a safe, fun way to find Web sites related to topics in this book. All of the sites on FactHound have been researched by our staff.

1. Visit *www.facthound.com*
2. Type in this special code: 1404837647
3. Click on the FETCH IT button.

Your trusty FactHound will fetch the best sites for you!

Look for all of the books in the Know Your Colors series:

| Autumn Orange |
| Batty for Black |
| Big Red Farm |
| Brown at the Zoo |
| Camping in Green |
| Hello, Yellow! |
| Pink Takes a Bow |
| Purple Pride |
| Splish, Splash, and Blue |
| Winter White |